18 most influential personalities

in the world and their works

Best book to achieve success in life

18 most influential personalities

in the world and their works

Best book to achieve success in life

DD BOOKS

Publishers for New Generations

Published by **DD Books**
Delhi, India
ddsalesglobal@gmail.com

Title: **18 Most Influential Personalities in the world and their Work**
Author: **Sarita Sharma and DD Books**

Price: **250/-**
Edition: **2024**

ISBN: **978-9359578866**

Contents

Forward

Welcome to a journey through the timeless wisdom of some of the most influential authors in the realm of personal development and success literature. This compilation brings together a rich tapestry of principles and insights from literary luminaries who have left an indelible mark on the genre.

At the forefront of this exploration is Napoleon Hill, a trailblazer whose seminal work, "**Think and Grow Rich**," has been a guiding light for generations of individuals aspiring to achieve personal and financial success. Hill's emphasis on definiteness of purpose and the transformative power of thought sets the stage for a transformative odyssey.

Dale Carnegie, another luminary in the self-help pantheon, invites readers to master the art of human relations in "**How to Win Friends and Influence People**." His principles, grounded in genuine human connection and effective communication, continue to be invaluable in both personal and professional spheres.

James Allen, through his timeless classic "**As a Man Thinketh**," imparts the profound idea that our thoughts shape our destiny. This slender volume serves as a philosophical cornerstone, urging readers to cultivate a positive and constructive mindset to influence their character and circumstances.

Charles F. Haanel's "**The Master Key System**" introduces a systematic approach to unlocking the latent powers of the mind and spirit. As you delve into the intricacies of mental forces, Haanel's work provides a blueprint for self-discovery and the unleashing of untapped potential.

"**The Richest Man in Babylon**" by George S. Clason takes us on a journey to ancient Babylon, where timeless principles of wealth-building and financial responsibility are woven into parables. Clason's wisdom transcends centuries, offering practical and enduring advice on managing one's finances and securing a prosperous future.

These are just a few among the luminaries featured in this compilation. From the empowering philosophy of Booker T. Washington's "**Up from Slavery**" to the entrepreneurial insights of P.T. Barnum's "**The Art of Money Getting**," each author and their masterpiece contribute a unique thread to the fabric of personal development.

Embark on this literary odyssey, and may the principles and insights within these classics illuminate your path toward personal transformation and success.

Happy reading and may your journey be as enriching as the wisdom contained within these timeless pages.

Napoleon Hill

Napoleon Hill

Napoleon Hill is a well-known figure in the field of self-help and personal development literature. His many books, such as "The Law of Success" and the classic "Think and Grow Rich," show his strong commitment to helping his readers grow and change.

What makes Hill's work special is that he goes beyond just giving advice and explores how the human mind works. He finds principles and strategies that can lead to success. His ideas are not just theories; they are things that can be put into practice to make real and lasting changes. His work is a trusted guide on the reader's journey, offering many insights that can change how they think and live.

In the vast world of self-help and personal development, Hill's work stands out as a treasure trove of valuable wisdom. His principles include the power of positive thinking, the power of clear goals, and the art of turning problems into advantages. Through his writing, readers not only learn things, but they also get practical tools to deal with life's challenges in a way that is strong, purposeful, and with a strong belief in their own abilities.

Napoleon Hill's legacy goes far beyond his books. It lives on in the minds and hearts of those he has inspired, and it continues to be a valuable and timeless guide for people who want to improve themselves and succeed in life.

Mastering Success through Napoleon Hill's 'Think and Grow Rich'

In his groundbreaking book "Think and Grow Rich," Napoleon Hill takes a deep dive into the human mind, revealing the extraordinary potential that lies untapped within each individual. Using the principles of positive thinking and goal setting, he creates a story that goes beyond financial success and provides a blueprint for a life filled with purpose and fulfillment.

The foundation of this transformative work is Hill's exploration of the power of positive thinking. He argues that when the mind is aligned with positivity and clarity, it becomes a powerful force that can shape one's destiny. The book serves as a guide for readers to tap into the unused potential of their thoughts, turning their aspirations into tangible achievements.

At the heart of Hill's philosophy is the art of setting goals. He carefully weaves the importance of clear goals throughout the story, emphasizing that a clear vision is the compass that guides individuals to success. Through anecdotes and principles, Hill illustrates how the simple act of setting goals can propel individuals to extraordinary heights, creating a roadmap for their ambitions.

"Think and Grow Rich" has become a cornerstone masterpiece in the self-help genre, laying the groundwork for countless later works. Its principles, rooted in positive thinking and goal setting, have become timeless pillars of personal development. Hill's insights, though written decades ago, continue to resonate with profound relevance in the ever-changing world of self-improvement.

"Think and Grow Rich" is more than just a book; it's a transformative journey into the depths of human potential. It challenges readers to rethink their approach to success, urging them to embrace the power of positive thinking and the precision of goal setting. As a beacon in the world of self-help literature, this book remains an essential guide for those seeking not only financial prosperity but a holistic and purposeful life.

Napoleon Hill's Principles of Success

At the core of Napoleon Hill's profound insights in "Think and Grow Rich" lies a single, invaluable success principle: the Definiteness of Purpose. This principle acts as the guiding star in the vast cosmos of personal achievement, extending beyond the pages of the book to become a beacon for those navigating the seas of ambition.

Hill passionately argues that success is not merely a product of vague desires; rather, it is the offspring of a clear, unwavering vision. The Definiteness of Purpose becomes the driving force that propels individuals forward, infusing every action with purpose and direction. It demands a meticulous articulation of one's goals, creating a laser-focused trajectory toward the desired outcome.

This principle becomes the linchpin for personal transformation. Hill emphasizes that individuals must not only dream big but also articulate their dreams with precision. The power lies not just in the desire but in the specificity of that desire. Through anecdotes and practical advice, Hill illustrates how a resolute purpose becomes the catalyst for overcoming obstacles, persisting through challenges, and ultimately achieving the envisioned success.

The Definiteness of Purpose is not a static concept but a dynamic force that shapes one's thoughts, actions, and decisions. Hill's work serves as a guide for readers to not only understand the importance of this principle but also to actively incorporate it into their lives. It is more than a success tip; it is a transformative philosophy that, when embraced, can unlock the extraordinary potential that lies within each individual.

Quote

In the pursuit of success, Napoleon Hill's wisdom stands as a guiding light, illuminating the path towards achieving our aspirations. Three of his profound quotes encapsulate the essence of his philosophy, emphasizing the power of the mind, the importance of desire, and the need for decisive action.

1. **"Whatever the mind of man can conceive and believe, it can achieve."**

This empowering quote underscores the immense potential of the human mind to shape reality. When we can envision our goals with clarity and believe wholeheartedly in their attainability, we lay the foundation for their manifestation. Our thoughts, our beliefs, our very imagination hold the power to transform our dreams into reality.

2. **"The starting point of all achievement is desire."**

Burning desire, an ardent passion for what we seek to accomplish, serves as the driving force behind every significant achievement. It is the flame that ignites our motivation, propelling us forward through obstacles and setbacks. Without a deep-seated yearning for our goals, we risk losing our momentum and succumbing to inertia. It is this intense desire that fuels our determination and perseverance, enabling us to overcome challenges and pursue our aspirations with unwavering resolve.

3. **"Don't wait. The time will never be just right."**

Procrastination, the nemesis of progress, often masquerades as prudence, waiting for the perfect conditions to materialize. However, Hill urges us to seize the moment, to take action decisively even when faced with uncertainty. True progress often lies beyond the realm of comfort and calculated risk, waiting to be embraced by those who dare to act. By embracing decisive action, we overcome the paralysis of analysis and embark on a journey towards our goals, embracing opportunities as they arise.

These three quotes, each a gem in Hill's treasure trove of wisdom, converge to form a powerful formula for success. By harnessing the power of belief, igniting our desires, and embracing decisive action, we open ourselves to a world of possibilities, where our dreams can take flight and our aspirations can find fulfillment. Hill's timeless principles serve as a beacon of inspiration, guiding us towards achieving our full potential and realizing our dreams.

James Allen

James Allen

In the field of self-help and personal development, James Allen stands out as a beacon of wisdom and inspiration. His remarkable work continues to guide readers toward significant growth, making him a high-quality author. His contributions to the field are truly extraordinary, serving as a valuable source of insights for those navigating the complexities of life.

James Allen's enduring legacy is rooted in his profound understanding of the human mind and spirit. His works, including the timeless classic "As a Man Thinketh," exemplify a rare combination of eloquence and depth, offering readers a roadmap to self-discovery and personal development. Allen's achievements extend beyond the realm of literature; they represent a commitment to nurturing the inner self, fostering a transformative journey toward a more fulfilling and purposeful life.

What sets Allen apart as a high-quality author is his ability to distill complex philosophical concepts into accessible and actionable principles. His writings are not merely theoretical; they are pragmatic guides that empower readers to take control of their thoughts and, consequently, their destinies. Allen's work becomes a trusted companion for those seeking not only success but a holistic and harmonious existence.

As readers engage with James Allen's writings, they find themselves immersed in a world of timeless wisdom and practical guidance.

His achievements extend beyond the pages of his books, resonating as a source of inspiration that transcends generations. In the realm of self-help and personal development, James Allen's work remains a cornerstone, a testament to the enduring impact of a high-quality author dedicated to the growth and well-being of those who seek the path of self-discovery.

Mastering Success through James Allen's "As a Man Thinketh"

In James Allen's timeless masterpiece, "As a Man Thinketh," he takes us on a profound journey to explore the transformative power of our thoughts. As a pioneer in the self-help literature genre, Allen crafts a story that delves into the essence of positive thinking and goal setting, laying the foundation for principles that would continue to be echoed in countless self-help teachings.

"As a Man Thinketh" opens a door into the intricate world of the human mind, where Allen masterfully conducts a symphony of thoughts. Through his eloquent prose, he unveils the concept that our thoughts are the architects of our destinies, shaping the circumstances of our lives. This foundational concept becomes the heart and soul of the book, resonating with readers on a profound level.

Central to Allen's philosophy is the alchemy of positive thinking. He argues that the mind is a fertile ground where seeds of positivity or negativity can take root, ultimately manifesting in one's reality. Allen urges readers to become vigilant guardians of their thoughts, recognizing the immense power they hold in shaping not only individual experiences but the course of one's entire life.

Woven into the fabric of "As a Man Thinketh" is the principle of goal setting as a guiding North Star. Allen emphasizes the importance of well-defined goals, portraying them as catalysts for personal development and achievement. According to Allen, goals serve as beacons that illuminate the path toward success, transforming vague aspirations into tangible realities.

Allen's insights, written over a century ago, continue to resonate as a timeless beacon that has guided the course of later self-help literature. His exploration of the interplay between thoughts, actions, and destiny lays the groundwork for principles embraced by countless authors who followed. "As a Man Thinketh" becomes not just a book but a cornerstone in the edifice of personal development literature.

James Allen's "As a Man Thinketh" is a masterpiece that transcends its time, offering readers a profound understanding of the transformative power of thoughts and the pivotal role of goal setting. It stands as a testament to the enduring relevance of positive thinking as a catalyst for personal growth and achievement, a beacon that continues to illuminate the path toward a more fulfilling and purposeful life.

James Allen's Principles of Success

Embedded within James Allen's profound teachings lies a singular and invaluable success principle: the Mastery of Thought. Allen asserts that the mind is the fertile ground from which all achievements spring forth, and thus, mastering one's thoughts becomes the cornerstone of ultimate success.

This principle emphasizes that the quality of one's thoughts directly influences the quality of one's life. Allen argues that a disciplined mind, cultivated through positive and constructive thinking, acts as a catalyst for transformative action. By consistently aligning thoughts with one's aspirations, individuals can shape their destinies, fostering a reality that reflects the harmony of their inner world.

In the quest for success, James Allen's Mastery of Thought principle serves as a guiding force, urging individuals to become conscious architects of their mental landscapes. By exercising control over thoughts, individuals gain the power to overcome obstacles, navigate challenges, and consistently move towards their goals. This principle goes beyond mere positive thinking; it advocates for the deliberate and disciplined cultivation of a mental environment conducive to success.

Allen's Mastery of Thought emerges as a timeless philosophy, resonating across the pages of "As a Man Thinketh" and extending its influence into the broader realm of personal development literature. It underscores the fundamental truth that success is not merely an external achievement but a reflection of one's internal state of mind.

The Mastery of thought principle encapsulates James Allen's core philosophy, offering readers a transformative key to unlock their fullest potential. It serves as a foundational principle for achieving success, not just in the conventional sense but as a holistic and harmonious alignment of one's thoughts with their desired outcomes.

Quote

"You are today where your thoughts have brought you; you will be tomorrow where your thoughts take you."

This quote emphasizes the critical role of our thoughts and mindset in shaping our present circumstances and future outcomes. It underscores the power of positive thinking and mindfulness in influencing the course of our lives.

"As a man thinketh in his heart, so is he."

Extracted from Allen's book "As a Man Thinketh," this quote highlights the deep connection between a person's thoughts and their character or destiny. It suggests that our inner thoughts shape our outward actions, ultimately determining our identity.

"Circumstances do not make a man, they reveal him."

In this quote, James Allen asserts that external circumstances do not define an individual; instead, they unveil one's true character. The quote encourages personal responsibility for reactions and responses to life's challenges, emphasizing character over external conditions.

James Allen's writings consistently revolve around the idea that our thoughts wield significant influence on our lives. By fostering positive and constructive thinking, individuals can intentionally shape their destinies in a positive direction.

Dale Carnegie

Dale Carnegie

Dale Carnegie emerges as a shining star in the field of personal development, embodying the essence of a high-quality author. His remarkable work and accomplishments bear witness to a lifelong dedication to fostering significant growth in individuals seeking self-help and personal development. Carnegie's contributions extend far beyond the realm of literature; they represent a profound investment in the empowerment of the human spirit.

Throughout his remarkable career, Carnegie has become synonymous with the art of effective communication, interpersonal skills, and personal growth. His groundbreaking work, including the timeless classic "How to Win Friends and Influence People," serves as a beacon for those navigating the complexities of self-improvement. Carnegie's insights are not mere words on a page; they are actionable principles that have propelled countless individuals toward personal and professional success.

Carnegie's approach is distinguished by its practicality and relevance, offering readers valuable tools to navigate the intricacies of life. His emphasis on effective communication, positive thinking, and the development of meaningful relationships has set a standard in the self-help genre. Carnegie's work is a testament to the idea that personal development is not just a solitary journey but a communal endeavor, where the ability to connect with others plays a pivotal role.

Dale Carnegie stands as a high-quality author whose work transcends time and resonates with readers seeking genuine, actionable guidance for personal development. His accomplishments reflect a commitment to developing valuable insights that not only inspire but also empower individuals to chart a course toward lasting growth and success.

Mastering Success through Dale Carnegie's "How to Win Friends and Influence People"

Dale Carnegie's masterpiece, "How to Win Friends and Influence People," is a practical guide to building positive connections and exerting influence through the power of positive thinking. Carnegie's insights go beyond mere strategies, offering fundamental principles that help readers understand how their thoughts shape their interactions with others.

Carnegie seamlessly transitions into the realm of effective communication, guiding readers through the intricacies of human interaction and demonstrating how positive thinking lays the foundation for meaningful connections. The book serves as a toolkit, providing practical advice on navigating conversations, building rapport, and leaving a lasting positive impression on others.

Goal setting plays a pivotal role in Carnegie's teachings, acting as a guiding light for his principles. The mastery of positive thinking aligns harmoniously with the pursuit of well-defined goals, creating a synergy that propels individuals toward success in their relationships, careers, and personal endeavors. Carnegie's principles, encapsulated in this book, transform from guidelines into transformative keys that unlock a world of positive influence.

"How to Win Friends and Influence People" transcends the boundaries of a mere book, becoming a beacon of timeless wisdom. It offers readers a comprehensive guide to cultivating positive influence through the mastery of positive thinking, effective communication, and the pursuit of meaningful goals.

Dale Carnegie's Principles of Success

Dale Carnegie's most valuable success principle, deeply embedded in his teachings, is the transformative power of understanding and empathizing with others. Carnegie emphasizes that true influence and success arise from authentic connections with people. This principle goes beyond mere transactions, highlighting the importance of positive, sincere relationships as the foundation for personal and professional fulfillment. Carnegie's philosophy underscores the profound impact of actively listening, understanding, and acknowledging the perspectives of those around us. By prioritizing empathy, individuals can forge meaningful connections that extend beyond superficial interactions. This principle serves as a guiding force, steering individuals away from self-centered pursuits and towards a collaborative and harmonious approach to achieving their goals. In Carnegie's world, success is not solely measured by personal achievements but by the ability to uplift and positively impact others. The principle of empathetic connection becomes a beacon for fostering goodwill, resolving conflicts, and building enduring relationships. Carnegie's work stands as a testament to the enduring truth that true success is not a solitary journey but a collaborative effort enriched by understanding and connecting with the aspirations and needs of those around us. At its core, Dale Carnegie's most valuable success principle encourages individuals to view success not in isolation but as a collective journey. By embracing empathy and understanding, individuals can navigate the complexities of human relationships, creating a ripple effect that extends far beyond personal accomplishments to contribute to the betterment of the wider community.

Quote

1. **"You can make more friends in two months by becoming interested in other people than you can in two years by trying to get other people interested in you."**

This quote underscores the significance of genuine interest in others as a key factor in building meaningful relationships. Dale Carnegie's teachings emphasize the value of understanding and connecting with people rather than focusing solely on self-promotion.

2. **"Success is getting what you want. Happiness is wanting what you get."**

Carnegie draws a distinction between success and happiness in this quote, suggesting that true fulfillment involves not just achieving external goals but also finding contentment in the present moment and appreciating what one has.

3. **"Inaction breeds doubt and fear. Action breeds confidence and courage. If you want to conquer fear, do not sit home and think about it. Go out and get busy."**

This quote encourages taking proactive steps to overcome fear and build confidence. Carnegie advocates for the transformative power of action and facing challenges directly, promoting a mindset of courage and confidence over succumbing to doubt and fear.

Dale Carnegie's principles consistently revolve around effective communication, interpersonal skills, and the profound importance of understanding and connecting with others. His approach to personal and professional success emphasizes building genuine relationships and taking purposeful action to achieve one's goals.

Orison Swett Marden

Orison Swett Marden

Orison Swett Marden stands out as a remarkable author, leaving an indelible mark on the field of self-help and personal development. His exceptional work reflects his deep commitment to inspiring and empowering individuals seeking to enhance their lives. Marden's contributions extend beyond the realm of ordinary literature, representing a visionary endeavor to uplift the human spirit.

In the vast expanse of self-help literature, Marden's works shine as beacons of wisdom and motivation. His influential titles, including "Pushing to the Front" and "An Iron Will," serve as comprehensive guides for readers on their path to self-discovery and personal growth. Marden's insights are not merely words on a page; they are transformative principles that hold the power to reshape individuals' perceptions and approaches to life.

Marden's unique ability to translate complex concepts into practical, actionable steps sets him apart as a high-quality author. His writings are not just motivational prose; they are blueprints for success, providing readers with tangible tools to conquer obstacles and cultivate a growth mindset. Through his work, Marden becomes a mentor, guiding individuals toward a life filled with purpose, resilience, and fulfillment.

Orison Swett Marden's legacy is one of enduring significance. His work continues to resonate across generations, offering timeless wisdom to those embarking on the journey of self-improvement. Marden's contributions serve as a testament to the enduring value of a high-quality author dedicated to the growth and well-being of those seeking to unlock their true potential.

Mastering Success through Orison Swett Marden's "Pushing to the Front"

Orison Swett Marden's "Pushing to the Front" stands as a shining star in the vast sea of self-help literature, a timeless guide that remains relevant beyond its era. In this literary gem, Marden skillfully interweaves the threads of positive thinking and goal setting, establishing the framework for principles that would become foundational for countless subsequent works in the realm of self-help.

Marden's journey begins with a symphony of positive thoughts, each page resonating with the power of a positive mindset. He emphasizes that the mind is not merely a battleground, but also a fertile ground where the seeds of success can be sown. Marden's insights become a transformative force, urging readers to recognize the profound impact of their thoughts on their path to self-improvement.

The principle of goal setting is seamlessly woven into the narrative, serving as a compass for success. Marden takes readers on a voyage into the significance of well-defined goals, illustrating how they act as beacons guiding individuals toward their desired destinations. The book transforms into a roadmap, demonstrating that the journey to the front demands not only positive thinking but also a clear vision of one's aspirations.

"Pushing to the Front" is more than a mere book; it is a foundational cornerstone upon which many later self-help principles have been built. Marden's exploration of positive thinking and goal setting becomes a timeless guide, offering readers not just insights but also actionable steps to push beyond obstacles and achieve personal and professional success.

Orison Swett Marden's "Pushing to the Front" is a literary masterpiece that transcends time, a testament to the enduring relevance of positive thinking and goal setting in the journey of self-improvement. It stands as a beacon, illuminating the path for readers to push to the forefront of their aspirations and forge a legacy of success.

Orison Swett Marden's Principles of Success

Orison Swett Marden's concept of the Power of Persistence is a timeless and invaluable principle that has inspired countless individuals to overcome challenges and achieve success. Marden's belief that persistence is not merely a virtue but the cornerstone of growth and accomplishment resonates deeply with those seeking to make their mark in the world.

At the heart of Marden's philosophy lies the unwavering conviction that tenacity, resilience, and an unyielding commitment to one's goals are the essential ingredients for success. He recognized that setbacks and obstacles are inevitable along the path to achieving one's dreams, but it is the persistent individual who possesses the strength and determination to rise above these challenges and emerge victorious.

Marden's assertion that every failure holds within it the seeds of equivalent success for those who persist in their efforts is a powerful testament to the transformative power of perseverance. He believed that failures, when viewed as learning opportunities rather than impediments, can serve as stepping stones towards greater achievements.

Marden's principle of persistence extends beyond a mere call to endure hardship. He advocated for cultivating a mindset of perseverance, encouraging individuals to embrace challenges as opportunities for growth and to press forward with determination even in the face of adversity. This mindset empowers individuals to transform obstacles into stepping stones towards their goals.

Marden's Power of Persistence serves as a guiding light for those navigating the complexities of life and seeking personal and professional fulfillment. His legacy extends far beyond the pages of his books, as his teachings continue to inspire individuals to push beyond their perceived limits, overcome challenges, and ultimately achieve their highest aspirations.

Quote

"Don't wait for extraordinary opportunities. Seize common occasions and make them great."

This quote encourages individuals to take advantage of everyday opportunities rather than waiting for something extraordinary. Marden believed in the transformative power of recognizing and maximizing the potential in ordinary situations.

"The greatest thing a man can do in this world is to make the most possible out of the stuff that has been given him."

Marden emphasizes the idea of maximizing one's potential and making the most of the resources and abilities that one possesses. This quote reflects his belief in personal development and self-improvement.

"The hopeful man sees success where others see failure, sunshine where others see shadows and storm."

This quote reflects Marden's positive and optimistic philosophy. It highlights the power of a hopeful and positive mindset in perceiving opportunities in challenges and finding success in what others might view as failure.

Orison Swett Marden's writings often focused on the principles of success, personal development, and the power of a positive mindset in overcoming challenges and achieving one's goals.

Russell Conwell

Russell Conwell

Russell Conwell's impact on the world of self-help and personal development is undeniable. His works, particularly the iconic lecture "Acres of Diamonds," have inspired generations of individuals to embrace their potential and pursue their dreams. Conwell's legacy lies in his ability to translate profound wisdom into practical and applicable principles, empowering readers to navigate life's challenges and achieve their goals.

Conwell's writings are not merely collections of words; they are transformative forces that ignite a spark of self-belief and determination within readers. He serves as a mentor, urging individuals to cultivate their talents, seize opportunities, and adopt a mindset of continuous growth. His ability to articulate complex ideas in a clear and engaging manner makes his works accessible to a wide audience, ensuring that his message of empowerment reaches those who need it most.

Russell Conwell's influence extends beyond the realm of self-help literature. His works have permeated popular culture, becoming cornerstones of motivational speeches and personal development seminars. His timeless messages of persistence, resilience, and the pursuit of excellence continue to resonate with individuals from all walks of life, inspiring them to overcome adversity and achieve their highest aspirations.

Conwell's legacy is one of empowerment, enlightenment, and enduring inspiration. His works serve as beacons of hope and guidance, illuminating the path for individuals seeking personal fulfillment and a life of purpose.

His contributions to the field of self-help and personal development remain invaluable, ensuring that his impact continues to shape the lives of countless individuals for generations to come.

Mastering Success through Russell Conwell's "Acres of Diamonds"

Russell Conwell's "Acres of Diamonds" is a timeless book that inspires readers to unlock their potential and achieve their dreams. The book is a captivating story that teaches readers the power of positive thinking and goal setting. Conwell's message is clear: we all have the potential to succeed, but we must first believe in ourselves and set clear goals.

One of the key takeaways from "Acres of Diamonds" is the importance of positive thinking. Conwell argues that we can attract success into our lives by focusing on the positive and believing in our ability to achieve our goals. He encourages readers to cultivate a mindset of abundance, believing that there are limitless opportunities available to us.

Another important principle in "Acres of Diamonds" is the importance of goal setting. Conwell argues that we need to have clear and specific goals in order to achieve them. He encourages readers to break down their goals into smaller, more manageable steps and to take action each day to move closer to their goals.

"Acres of Diamonds" is a timeless classic that has inspired generations of readers. Conwell's message of positive thinking and goal setting is still relevant today, and his book is a valuable resource for anyone who wants to achieve their full potential.

Russell Conwell's Principles of Success

In his teachings, Russell Conwell emphasizes the importance of recognizing opportunities as the key to success. He believes that success is not an unattainable goal but rather a series of disguised challenges waiting to be identified and seized. Conwell's philosophy revolves around the notion that every situation, no matter how mundane, holds the potential for significant growth and accomplishment.

Conwell encourages readers to cultivate a heightened sense of awareness, enabling them to see beyond the surface of challenges and setbacks. He highlights the transformative power of recognizing opportunities within one's immediate surroundings, which he metaphorically refers to as the "Acres of Diamonds" within reach. This keen awareness serves as a guiding light for individuals on their journey to success.

Embedded within this principle is the understanding that every experience, encounter, and setback carries the potential for opportunity. By adopting a mindset attuned to identifying and maximizing these opportunities, individuals can navigate their paths with intention and resilience. Conwell's teachings serve as a call to action, urging readers not to seek success in distant horizons but to recognize the wealth of possibilities that lie within their current circumstances.

The "Value of Opportunity Recognition" becomes a transformative key, unlocking the doors to personal and professional fulfillment. Conwell's legacy lies not only in the words he imparts but also in the actionable principle he instills – a principle that transcends time and continues to inspire individuals to identify, seize, and cultivate the opportunities that pave the way for a life of purpose and achievement.

Quote

"Your diamonds are not in far distant mountains or in yonder seas; they are in your own backyard, if you but dig for them."

This quote encapsulates the central theme of Conwell's famous lecture. He encourages individuals to recognize the potential for success and wealth in their immediate surroundings rather than seeking it in distant places.

"Money is power, and you ought to be reasonably ambitious to have it. You ought because you can do more good with it than you could without it."

Conwell believed in the positive impact that individuals could have by acquiring wealth and using it for benevolent purposes. This quote reflects his perspective on the potential for good that comes with financial success.

"Greatness consists not in the holding of some future office, but really consists in doing great deeds with little means and the accomplishment of vast purposes from the private ranks of life."

Conwell emphasizes the idea that greatness is not necessarily tied to holding a prominent position but is rather achieved through meaningful actions and accomplishments, even with limited resources.

Russell Conwell's teachings often revolved around the themes of seizing opportunities, the value of hard work, and the potential for success that exists within one's own circumstances.

Florence Scovel Shinn

Florence Scovel Shinn

Florence Scovel Shinn stands as an exceptional author whose remarkable work has become a beacon in the realm of self-help and personal development. Her achievements are marked by a profound dedication to promoting significant individual growth, providing invaluable insights and principles for cultivating a more fulfilling and purposeful life.

Shinn's notable works, including "The Game of Life and How to Play It," "Your Word is Your Wand," and "The Secret Door to Success," represent a treasure trove of timeless wisdom. Through her eloquent prose and practical teachings, Shinn imparts transformative lessons, encouraging readers to grasp the power they hold in shaping their destinies through thoughts and words.

What distinguishes Shinn as an exceptional author is her ability to seamlessly blend spirituality, metaphysics, and practicality into a harmonious narrative. Her writings go beyond mere motivational rhetoric, providing readers with actionable steps to manifest positive change in their lives. Shinn becomes a guide, steering individuals toward self-discovery, empowerment, and the realization of their true potential.

Shinn's legacy extends beyond the pages of her books, evident in the enduring impact her teachings have on those seeking personal and spiritual growth. She becomes a mentor through her work, offering readers a roadmap to navigate life's complexities, make conscious choices, and cultivate a mindset that attracts abundance, success, and joy.

Florence Scovel Shinn's contributions as an exceptional author resonate as a timeless source of inspiration and guidance. Her remarkable work continues to be a wellspring of wisdom for individuals embarking on the journey of self-discovery and personal development, fostering a legacy of empowerment that transcends generations.

Mastering Success through Florence Scovel Shinn's "The Game of Life and How to Play It"

In her seminal work, "The Game of Life and How to Play It," Florence Scovel Shinn invites readers to embark on a profound exploration of the principles that govern our existence. This timeless masterpiece serves as a roadmap for those seeking to navigate the realms of positive thinking and goal setting, essential elements in the intricate game of life.

Shinn unveils the secrets of this cosmic game by revealing the immense power of our thoughts, positioning us as players on a cosmic chessboard. The opening moves involve recognizing the profound influence of our words and beliefs, setting the stage for a transformative journey of self-discovery.

Seamlessly interwoven into the narrative is the principle of positive thinking as the ultimate game-changer. Shinn imparts the wisdom that our thoughts are potent seeds, capable of cultivating a life brimming with joy and fulfillment. Her book becomes a practical manual, guiding readers in mastering the art of channeling thoughts to manifest desired outcomes in the grand game of life.

Delving into the masterstroke of goal setting, Shinn portrays it as the guiding compass directing our moves in the game. She illuminates the significance of well-defined goals, serving as beacons illuminating the path toward individual destinies. In the cosmic game of life, goal setting emerges as the strategic maneuver aligning actions with aspirations.

"The Game of Life and How to Play It" has evolved into a foundational cornerstone for subsequent self-help literature. Shinn's insights, rooted in the power of positive thinking and goal setting, continue to echo through time, inspiring countless authors. Her teachings transcend mere guidance, transforming into a timeless manual for unlocking the secrets of personal and spiritual growth.

Florence Scovel Shinn's book transcends its status as a guide, elevating itself to a philosophical masterpiece that resonates with readers. It offers profound lessons on the intricate art of playing the game of life with wisdom, purpose, and boundless positivity.

Florence Scovel Shinn's Principles of Success

Florence Scovel Shinn introduces the transformative Principle of Divine Alignment, a beacon guiding individuals on their path towards fulfillment and success. At the heart of Shinn's teachings lies the concept that aligning one's thoughts, beliefs, and actions with divine principles unlocks the gateway to true success.

In Shinn's philosophy, the Principle of Divine Alignment emphasizes the importance of harmonizing one's intentions with higher, universal truths. By grasping and embodying these timeless principles, individuals can navigate life's complexities with clarity, purpose, and unwavering faith.

This principle challenges individuals to step beyond the confines of conventional thinking and connect with a higher, divine wisdom. Shinn asserts that success is not solely attained through personal effort but rather a collaborative process with the divine forces at play. By aligning one's goals and aspirations with the universal laws of abundance, individuals open themselves to a vast realm of possibilities.

Furthermore, Shinn underscores the significance of affirmations and the power of the spoken word in achieving divine alignment. The words we choose to utter have a profound impact on our reality, shaping our experiences. By consciously employing positive affirmations aligned with divine principles, individuals can manifest the success they desire.

Florence Scovel Shinn's Principle of Divine Alignment serves as a guiding light for those traversing the journey of success. It invites individuals to transcend the ordinary and embrace a co-creative partnership with higher, universal forces. This principle, woven into the fabric of her teachings, continues to inspire readers to align their thoughts and actions with divine wisdom, unlocking the doors to a life of purpose, abundance, and enduring success.

Quote

"Your word is your wand. The words you speak create your own destiny."

Shinn emphasizes the power of words in shaping one's reality. This quote suggests that the language we use and the thoughts we express have a direct impact on the course of our lives.

"You will be a failure, until you impress the subconscious with the conviction you are a success. This is done by making an affirmation which 'clicks.'"

Shinn believed in the importance of affirmations and the role of the subconscious mind in shaping one's experiences. This quote underscores the idea that creating a deep conviction of success within the subconscious is crucial for achieving one's goals.

"Every great work, every big accomplishment, has been brought into manifestation through holding to the vision, and often just before the big achievement, comes apparent failure and discouragement."

Shinn's perspective on perseverance and vision is reflected in this quote. It suggests that challenges and setbacks may occur just before significant achievements, and maintaining a clear vision is essential for overcoming obstacles.

Florence Scovel Shinn's teachings often centered around the idea of the power of thought, affirmations, and the role of spirituality in achieving success and fulfillment.

❁❁❁

Ralph Waldo Emerson

Ralph Waldo Emerson

Ralph Waldo Emerson stands as a preeminent author, leaving an indelible mark on the realm of self-help and personal development. His remarkable work bears witness to a deep-seated commitment to nurturing significant growth in individuals, offering them invaluable insights and principles to cultivate a more fulfilling and meaningful life.

Emerson's influential essays, including "Self-Reliance" and "The Oversoul," transcend the boundaries of time, serving as beacons of wisdom for readers seeking to navigate life's complexities. His achievements extend beyond the realm of conventional literature, representing a visionary investment in empowering the human spirit.

What sets Emerson apart as an exceptional author is his ability to seamlessly blend philosophical depth with practical guidance. His writings are not mere intellectual exercises; they are transformative principles that possess the potential to reshape the way individuals perceive and navigate their lives. Emerson emerges as a guide, urging readers to delve into their inner resources, trust their intuition, and embark on a journey of self-discovery.

Emerson's legacy is one of enduring significance. His work continues to resonate across generations, providing timeless wisdom for those embarking on the path of self-improvement. His contributions stand as a testament to the enduring value of a high-quality author committed to the development and well-being of those who seek to unlock their true potential.

Mastering Success through Ralph Waldo Emerson's "Self-Reliance"

In his groundbreaking work, "Self-Reliance," Ralph Waldo Emerson beckons readers to embark on a transformative journey, unveiling the profound principles that shape a life of authenticity and fulfillment. This literary gem transcends the boundaries of a mere book, establishing itself as a timeless guide that laid the foundation for much of what later became the cornerstone of self-help literature.

Emerson's "Self-Reliance" opens with a resounding call to individualism, challenging readers to break free from the shackles of societal conformity and embrace the uniqueness of their own minds. He urges individuals to forge their paths with unwavering confidence and self-assurance, trusting their intuition as a compass to guide them towards their true selves.

Woven into the fabric of Emerson's philosophy is the transformative power of positive thinking, a timeless principle that continues to resonate through the corridors of self-help literature. "Self-Reliance" encourages readers to cultivate a positive mindset, emphasizing that optimism and self-belief are fundamental catalysts for personal growth and success.

Emerson's teachings seamlessly integrate the concept of goal setting as an expression of self-reliance. He contends that individuals, by trusting their inner convictions, can set meaningful goals aligned with their authentic selves. These goals become not only benchmarks for success but also powerful affirmations of one's individuality and purpose.

"Self-Reliance" stands as a foundational cornerstone for later self-help literature, setting the stage for principles that endure through time. Emerson's insights, rooted in the power of positive thinking and goal setting, continue to inspire countless authors who have followed in his footsteps. His work is not just a guide; it is a philosophical masterpiece that transcends its era, offering timeless wisdom that empowers individuals to embark on a journey of self-discovery and authenticity.

Ralph Waldo Emerson's Principles of Success

Ralph Waldo Emerson leaves readers with a timeless and invaluable success principle—the Sovereignty of Individuality. At the core of Emerson's philosophy lies the profound idea that true success is intimately connected to embracing one's unique identity and forging an authentic path in the world.

Emerson asserts that the key to realizing one's full potential lies in cultivating a deep sense of individuality. The success principle he imparts is not a call to conform to societal expectations but a resounding invitation to express one's authentic self with boldness. In this philosophy, true success is not measured by external validation but by the alignment of one's actions with the inner compass of individuality.

The Sovereignty of Individuality emerges as a guiding light for navigating life's intricacies. Emerson encourages readers to trust their intuition, celebrate their distinctiveness, and resist the pressures of conformity. By doing so, individuals tap into an endless reservoir of creativity, resilience, and authenticity—the foundational elements of genuine success.

Emerson's success principle reverberates through time, transcending the ever-changing landscapes of achievement. It challenges individuals to define success on their own terms, rooted in the authentic expression of their passions and values. The Sovereignty of Individuality becomes a transformative key, unlocking the doors to a life rich in purpose, fulfillment, and enduring success.

Ralph Waldo Emerson's success principle serves as a profound reminder that the path to true success is paved with the authenticity of one's individuality. It stands as an enduring beacon, inspiring generations to embrace their uniqueness and navigate the journey of success with the unwavering confidence that comes from living a life true to oneself.

Quote

"Do not go where the path may lead, go instead where there is no path and leave a trail."

This quote encourages individuals to embrace individuality and take their own unique paths in life. Emerson emphasizes the value of forging new ways and leaving a mark rather than simply following established routes.

"What lies behind us and what lies before us are tiny matters compared to what lies within us."

Emerson highlights the importance of inner strength and character in facing life's challenges. This quote suggests that our internal resources and capabilities are more significant than external circumstances.

"To be yourself in a world that is constantly trying to make you something else is the greatest accomplishment."

Emerson advocates for authenticity and self-expression. This quote encourages individuals to resist societal pressures and expectations, emphasizing the importance of staying true to one's identity.

Ralph Waldo Emerson's writings often explored themes of individualism, self-reliance, and the inherent goodness of people. His philosophical ideas had a profound impact on American literature and thought during the 19th century.

Harriet Martineau

Harriet Martineau

Harriet Martineau stands as an exceptional author whose remarkable work has left an indelible mark on the landscape of self-help and personal development. Her achievements bear witness to a deep-seated commitment to nurturing significant growth in individuals, offering them invaluable insights and principles to cultivate a more fulfilling and purposeful life.

Martineau's literary contributions, including "How to Observe Morals and Manners" and "Illustrations of Political Economy," transcend the limitations of time. Through her eloquent prose and astute observations, she emerges as a guiding force in the realm of self-help, providing readers with practical tools for self-improvement.

What distinguishes Martineau as an exceptional author is her ability to seamlessly blend societal observations with personal development principles. Her writings serve not only as a mirror reflecting the intricacies of human behavior but also as a source of wisdom for individuals seeking personal growth. Martineau becomes a mentor, urging readers to examine their morals and manners, fostering a deep understanding of the self.

Martineau's legacy extends beyond the words on the page, evident in the transformative impact her work has on those who engage with it. She becomes a beacon for readers navigating the complexities of life, offering valuable insights into human behavior, societal dynamics, and the path to personal development.

Harriet Martineau's contributions as an exceptional author resonate as a timeless source of inspiration and guidance. Her remarkable work continues to be a wellspring of wisdom for individuals embarking on the journey of self-discovery and personal development, fostering a legacy of empowerment that transcends generations.

Mastering Success through Harriet Martineau's "How to Observe Morals and Manners"

In her captivating work, "How to Observe Morals and Manners," Harriet Martineau takes readers on a journey that extends beyond mere observation, transforming into a timeless guide for personal development. Within its pages, Martineau delves into the intricate workings of human behavior, establishing a foundation for principles that continue to resonate through the corridors of later self-help literature.

In this literary masterpiece, Martineau emerges as a keen observer of societal dynamics, providing readers with a unique lens through which to navigate the complexities of human interaction. Her work transcends the boundaries of a mere sociological study, evolving into a practical manual for personal growth. Martineau draws parallels between societal observations and foundational self-help principles, offering readers valuable insights into the transformative power of positive thinking.

As Martineau explores the intricacies of morals and manners, she uncovers the profound impact of a positive mindset on individual and societal well-being. She becomes a pioneer in linking the nuances of human behavior to the foundational principle that optimism and positive thought are catalysts for personal development. Her work paves the way for later self-help literature, emphasizing the importance of aligning personal goals with societal values.

"How to Observe Morals and Manners" stands as a cornerstone for subsequent self-help literature, its insights rippling through time. Martineau's unique blend of societal observation and personal development principles provides readers with a roadmap for navigating the intricacies of human behavior. Her work transcends the realm of sociological exploration, becoming a timeless guide for those seeking personal growth and understanding.

Harriet Martineau's book elevates itself beyond its role as a societal commentary, transforming into a beacon for readers on the path of personal development. "How to Observe Morals and Manners" offers profound insights into the power of positive thinking, goal setting, and the intricate dance between individual growth and societal norms.

Harriet Martineau's Harriet Martineau

Harriet Martineau introduces the profound and enduring success principle of Observational Wisdom. At the heart of Martineau's philosophy lies the concept that keen observation of morals and manners serves as a powerful tool for personal and societal advancement.

Martineau challenges individuals to cultivate the habit of thoughtful observation, urging them to scrutinize the intricacies of human behavior and societal norms. The success principle she imparts is grounded in the belief that a deep understanding of these dynamics provides a strategic advantage in navigating life's complexities.

The Principle of Observational Wisdom becomes a transformative key for personal growth. Martineau encourages readers to develop a heightened awareness of their surroundings, fostering the ability to discern patterns, motivations, and societal trends. This acute observational skill, she contends, is the foundation for making informed decisions and charting a course toward success.

Moreover, Martineau's success principle underscores the importance of applying observational insights to personal development. By understanding the dynamics of morals and manners, individuals can align their goals and aspirations with societal values, creating a harmonious path to success.

Harriet Martineau's Principle of Observational Wisdom becomes a guiding light for those seeking success. It invites individuals to sharpen their observational acumen, offering a unique vantage point for personal and professional growth. This principle, woven into the fabric of her teachings, continues to inspire readers to embrace the transformative power of keen observation as they navigate the journey toward enduring success.

Quote

"The life of a wise man is a commentary on the past."

Martineau suggests that a wise person's life serves as a reflection and interpretation of past experiences. This quote underscores the idea that individuals can learn and gain wisdom from their own life experiences.

"To judge wisely, we must know how things appear to the unwise."

Martineau emphasizes the importance of empathy and understanding different perspectives. This quote suggests that true wisdom comes from being able to see and comprehend situations from the viewpoint of those who may not have the same level of insight.

"The sense of being well-dressed gives a feeling of inward tranquility which religion is powerless to bestow."

Martineau acknowledges the psychological impact of personal appearance and suggests that feeling well-dressed can contribute to a sense of inner peace and confidence.

Harriet Martineau's work focused on issues of social justice, equality, and the examination of societal structures. As one of the earliest sociologists, she made significant contributions to the understanding of social issues and their impact on individuals and communities.

Samuel Smiles

Samuel Smiles

Samuel Smiles emerges as an exceptional author, celebrated for his remarkable work and profound contributions to the realms of self-help and personal development. His literary legacy stands as a testament to a deep-seated commitment to fostering significant growth in individuals, offering them invaluable insights and principles to cultivate a life of enduring value.

Through seminal works such as "Self-Help" and "Character," Smiles becomes a beacon for readers seeking to navigate the complexities of personal development. His achievements extend beyond the boundaries of conventional literature, representing a visionary investment in empowering individuals to take charge of their destinies.

What distinguishes Smiles as an exceptional author is his unique ability to seamlessly blend practical wisdom with philosophical depth. His writings transcend the realm of mere advice, evolving into transformative principles that resonate through the ages. Smiles assumes the role of a mentor, guiding readers on a journey of self-discovery and imparting lessons that extend far beyond the pages of his books.

Smiles' legacy is not confined to a specific era; it transcends time, inspiring generations with a timeless message of self-reliance, diligence, and the pursuit of excellence. His work remains a wellspring of guidance for those seeking to unlock their true potential and lead lives of purpose and fulfillment.

Samuel Smiles' contributions as an exceptional author represent a legacy of empowerment. His remarkable work continues to be a source of inspiration and wisdom, providing readers with the tools they need to chart a course toward personal development and cultivate enduring value in their lives.

Mastering Success through Samuel Smiles's "Self-Help"

In his timeless classic "Self-Help," Samuel Smiles invites readers on a transformative journey, laying the foundation for principles that continue to echo through the corridors of later self-help literature. This literary masterpiece not only serves as a beacon for personal development but also sets the stage for a profound exploration of the power of positive thinking and goal setting.

"Self-Help" emerges as a pioneer in the self-help genre, a groundbreaking work that transcends its era to become a guiding light for generations to come. Samuel Smiles stands as a trailblazer, boldly advocating for the idea that individuals possess the agency to shape their destinies through self-reliance and determination.

Woven into the fabric of "Self-Help" is the transformative power of positive thinking. Smiles becomes an early proponent of the notion that cultivating a positive mindset is the cornerstone of personal development. His insights lay the foundation for later self-help luminaries who expound on the profound impact of optimism on one's journey toward success.

"Self-Help" introduces the concept of goal setting as a catalyst for personal achievement. Smiles contends that individuals, armed with a clear vision of their aspirations, can navigate the complexities of life with purpose and determination. His teachings become a timeless manual for those seeking to align their actions with their ambitions.

The principles outlined in "Self-Help" become foundational for later self-help literature, shaping the discourse on personal development for decades. Smiles' work becomes not just a book but a cornerstone, inspiring countless authors who follow in his footsteps. The enduring relevance of his insights speaks to the timeless nature of the principles he espouses.

"Self-Help" is more than a book; it is a transformative guide that empowers individuals to embark on a journey of self-discovery and growth. Samuel Smiles' legacy resonates through the pages, offering profound insights into the power of positive thinking, goal setting, and the enduring principles that continue to guide readers toward a life of self-determined success.

Samuel Smiles's Principles of Success

In his enduring work, Samuel Smiles imparts a timeless and invaluable success principle—the Principle of Self-Reliance. At the core of Smiles' philosophy lies the profound idea that true success is inextricably linked to an individual's ability to depend on their own capabilities, determination, and resourcefulness.

The Principle of Self-Reliance challenges individuals to take charge of their destinies, emphasizing the transformative power that arises from relying on their own skills and initiative. Smiles asserts that by cultivating a strong sense of self-reliance, individuals not only navigate challenges more effectively but also become the architects of their own success.

Furthermore, Smiles underscores the significance of personal responsibility within the Principle of Self-Reliance. He encourages individuals to take ownership of their actions, decisions, and life paths. By doing so, they harness the power to shape their destinies and overcome obstacles with resilience and determination.

The Principle of Self-Reliance emerges as a guiding light for those seeking success, urging individuals to trust in their abilities, persevere in the face of adversity, and chart a course aligned with their aspirations. Smiles' wisdom extends beyond a mere call for independence; it becomes a transformative key unlocking the doors to a life of purpose, achievement, and enduring success.

Samuel Smiles' Principle of Self-Reliance remains a cornerstone for those navigating the journey of success. It serves as a profound reminder that, in the pursuit of one's goals, the strength to succeed lies within, waiting to be unleashed through an unwavering commitment to self-reliance and personal responsibility.

Quote

"He who never made a mistake, never made a discovery."

This quote emphasizes the idea that making mistakes is an inherent part of the process of discovery and learning. Smiles suggests that taking risks and learning from failures are essential components of success.

"Self-help is the best help."

One of Smiles' central themes is the idea that individuals have the power to improve their lives through their own efforts. This quote underscores the importance of self-reliance and taking proactive steps toward personal development.

"Hope is like the sun, which, as we journey toward it, casts the shadow of our burden behind us."

Smiles uses the metaphor of hope as a guiding force that, as we move toward it, lightens the burden of our challenges. This quote reflects his optimistic perspective on the power of hope to transform one's outlook.

Samuel Smiles' most famous work is "Self-Help," published in 1859, which had a significant impact on the self-improvement genre. His writings encouraged individuals to take responsibility for their own lives and to believe in their capacity for self-improvement.

❁❁❁

Lyman Abbott

Lyman Abbott

Lyman Abbott emerges as an exceptional author, leaving an indelible mark through his remarkable work and notable achievements in the realms of self-help and personal development. His literary contributions stand as a testament to a steadfast commitment to fostering significant growth in readers, providing them with valuable insights and principles that cultivate a path of personal development and self-discovery.

Abbott's work transcends the boundaries of conventional literature, becoming a beacon for those seeking guidance in navigating the complexities of life. Whether through philosophical reflections, insightful essays, or practical advice, Abbott's writings become a source of inspiration and empowerment for individuals on their journey toward personal growth.

What distinguishes Abbott as an exceptional author is not only the depth of his insights but also his unique ability to connect with readers on a personal level. His works serve as more than just written words; they become companions on the path to self-improvement, offering wisdom and encouragement to those navigating the challenges of personal development.

Abbott's legacy extends beyond the literary realm, evident in the transformative impact his work has on the lives of readers. His achievements become a touchstone for individuals seeking to understand themselves better, overcome obstacles, and chart a course toward a more fulfilling and purposeful life.

Lyman Abbott's contributions as an exceptional author resonate as a legacy of empowerment and enlightenment. His remarkable work continues to be a source of valuable guidance, inspiring readers to embark on a journey of self-discovery and personal development, fostering a legacy of growth that transcends the pages of his writings.

Mastering Success through Lyman Abbott's "The Evolution of Christianity"

In his groundbreaking work, "The Evolution of Christianity," Lyman Abbott invites readers to embark on a profound journey through the historical and philosophical dimensions of the Christian faith. While the book delves into the intricate evolution of religious thought, it subtly interweaves principles that resonate with the foundations of later self-help literature, particularly emphasizing the transformative power of positive thinking and goal setting.

Abbott's exploration of the evolution of Christianity serves as a gateway to unlocking spiritual wisdom. The book becomes a tapestry woven with insights from historical narratives and religious philosophy, inviting readers to contemplate the transformative power embedded in spiritual evolution.

Embedded within the narrative is the subtle yet powerful theme of positive thinking. Abbott draws connections between the evolution of Christian thought and the empowering concept of maintaining a positive mindset. The book encourages readers to recognize the optimistic undercurrents in spiritual evolution and harness the strength derived from positive perspectives in their own lives.

As the narrative unfolds, Abbott skillfully weaves the concept of goal setting into the fabric of spiritual evolution. Readers are prompted to reflect on the aspirations of the Christian faith and, by extension, set personal and spiritual goals. The book becomes a guide for aligning individual aspirations with the enduring principles embedded in the evolution of Christianity.

"The Evolution of Christianity" emerges as a bridge between faith and personal development. Abbott's exploration of spiritual growth seamlessly aligns with principles found in later self-help literature, elevating the book beyond a mere historical narrative. It becomes a unique guide for readers seeking not only a deeper understanding of Christianity but also insights into the timeless principles that nurture personal and spiritual development.

Lyman Abbott's "The Evolution of Christianity" transcends its role as a historical narrative. It becomes a portal for readers to explore the interplay between spiritual evolution, positive thinking, and goal setting—an intricate tapestry that continues to resonate as a source of inspiration for those seeking both faith-based insights and personal development principles.

Lyman Abbott's Principles of Success

In his profound work, Lyman Abbott imparts an enduring success principle—the Principle of Harmonious Growth. At the heart of Abbott's philosophy lies the idea that true success extends beyond mere individual achievement. It encompasses the holistic development of one's mind, body, and spirit, fostering a harmonious coexistence with the world around us.

The Principle of Harmonious Growth challenges individuals to view success as a comprehensive journey, one that embraces intellectual, emotional, and spiritual dimensions. Abbott asserts that the pursuit of success should not be an isolated endeavor but rather seamlessly integrated into a balanced and harmonious life, where personal growth aligns with societal well-being.

Furthermore, Abbott emphasizes the significance of aligning personal aspirations with a broader sense of purpose and service to others. The success principle he imparts encourages individuals to find fulfillment not only in personal achievements but also in contributing positively to the collective growth and welfare of society.

The Principle of Harmonious Growth emerges as a transformative guide for those seeking success, urging individuals to cultivate a well-rounded and interconnected approach to personal development. Abbott's wisdom extends beyond the traditional definition of success, offering a nuanced perspective that encompasses the flourishing of the individual within the context of a harmonious and interconnected world.

Lyman Abbott's Principle of Harmonious Growth remains a timeless beacon for those navigating the journey of success. It serves as a profound reminder that genuine success is achieved not in isolation but through a holistic and harmonious pursuit of personal and societal well-being, fostering a legacy of balanced growth that continues to resonate through the ages.

Quote

"Do not teach your children never to be angry; teach them how to be angry."

Abbott emphasizes the importance of helping children understand and manage their emotions, including anger. Instead of suppressing emotions, he suggests teaching healthy ways to express and handle them.

"The world is not a place for optimists. The world is not a place for pessimists. The world is a place for realists."

Abbott advocates for a realistic perspective on life. This quote suggests that acknowledging both the challenges and opportunities in the world is essential for navigating it effectively.

"One of the hardest things in life is having words in your heart that you can't utter."

This quote speaks to the challenges of unexpressed feelings or thoughts. Abbott reflects on the difficulty of holding emotions inside without being able to communicate them.

Lyman Abbott was known for his work as an editor of "The Outlook" magazine and for his progressive views on theology and social issues. His writings often reflected a thoughtful and humane approach to understanding and engaging with the complexities of life.

Elbert Hubbard

Elbert Hubbard

Elbert Hubbard stands as an exceptional author, celebrated for his remarkable work and profound contributions to the realms of self-help and personal development. His literary legacy stands as a testament to a deep-seated commitment to fostering significant growth in readers, providing them with invaluable insights and principles that serve as catalysts for personal transformation and development.

Hubbard's work transcends the boundaries of conventional literature, representing a beacon for individuals navigating the complexities of self-help and personal growth. His achievements extend beyond mere written words, encompassing a visionary investment in empowering readers to cultivate lives of enduring value and purpose.

What distinguishes Hubbard as an exceptional author is not only the depth of his insights but also his unique ability to connect with readers on a personal level. His works become more than just words on a page; they transform into companions on the journey of self-improvement, offering wisdom, encouragement, and actionable guidance to those seeking to enhance their lives.

Hubbard's legacy is not confined to a specific era; it resonates through time, inspiring generations with a timeless message of self-reliance, determination, and the pursuit of excellence. His work remains a source of guidance for those striving to unlock their true potential and lead lives of purpose, enriched by the valuable principles embedded in Hubbard's writings.

Elbert Hubbard's contributions as an exceptional author represent a legacy of empowerment and enlightenment. His remarkable work continues to be a wellspring of inspiration, providing readers with the tools they need to navigate the journey of self-help and personal development, fostering a legacy of growth that extends far beyond the pages of his writings.

Mastering Success through Elbert Hubbard's "A Message to Garcia"

In his inspiring work "A Message to Garcia," Elbert Hubbard invites readers to embark on a journey of unwavering determination and resolute action. While not explicitly focused on positive thinking and goal setting, this timeless work subtly weaves in principles that laid the foundation for later self-help literature, emphasizing the power of a positive mindset and the pursuit of clearly defined objectives.

"A Message to Garcia" begins with a compelling call to action, recounting a critical mission during the Spanish-American War. Hubbard uses this narrative as a metaphor for the importance of initiative, responsibility, and the ability to execute tasks without hesitation or unnecessary complexity.

Embedded within the narrative is the theme of positive thinking—an underlying current that propels the protagonist, Rowan, to accept a seemingly impossible mission with unwavering optimism. Hubbard subtly underscores the transformative power of maintaining a positive mindset, even in the face of daunting challenges.

At the heart of the message lies the protagonist's unwavering commitment to delivering the message to Garcia. This unwavering resolve becomes a metaphor for goal setting, as readers are encouraged to define their objectives with clarity and pursue them with a tenacity that knows no bounds.

While not overtly a treatise on positive thinking and goal setting, "A Message to Garcia" emerges as a parable that lays the groundwork for later self-help literature. Hubbard's narrative becomes a timeless lesson on the importance of initiative, a positive mindset, and resolute pursuit of goals—principles that resonate through the corridors of self-help wisdom.

"A Message to Garcia" serves as a unique entry point into the realm of self-help, where the principles of positive thinking and goal setting are woven into the fabric of a narrative that inspires readers to embrace initiative, responsibility, and unwavering resolve in the pursuit of their objectives.

Elbert Hubbard's Principles of Success

Elbert Hubbard imparts a unique and invaluable success principle—the Principle of Initiative. At the heart of Hubbard's philosophy lies the profound idea that true success is inextricably linked to an individual's ability to seize the initiative, embrace responsibility, and execute tasks with unwavering determination.

The Principle of Initiative challenges individuals to be proactive and self-reliant in their pursuits. Hubbard asserts that genuine success is not a passive endeavor but rather a consequence of taking the initiative to identify opportunities, shoulder responsibilities, and navigate challenges with a proactive mindset.

Furthermore, Hubbard emphasizes the significance of a sense of responsibility within the Principle of Initiative. He encourages individuals to approach tasks and goals with a deep sense of accountability, recognizing that success is not merely about achieving personal aims but also about contributing positively to the broader context of one's responsibilities.

The Principle of Initiative emerges as a transformative guide for those seeking success, urging individuals to embrace a proactive and responsible approach to their endeavors. Hubbard's wisdom extends beyond a mere call for action; it becomes a key unlocking the doors to a life of purpose, achievement, and enduring success.

Elbert Hubbard's Principle of Initiative remains a cornerstone for those navigating the journey of success. It serves as a profound reminder that, in the pursuit of one's goals, the ability to take initiative, assume responsibility, and execute tasks with determination are fundamental keys to unlocking a path toward a life of meaningful accomplishment.

Quote

"Do not take life too seriously. You will never get out of it alive."

This quote reflects Hubbard's wit and humor. It suggests that life is meant to be lived with a sense of lightheartedness and not to be taken overly seriously.

"The best preparation for good work tomorrow is to do good work today."

Hubbard emphasizes the importance of consistently doing one's best in the present as a preparation for future success. This quote encourages a proactive and diligent approach to work.

"The world is moving so fast these days that the man who says it can't be done is generally interrupted by someone doing it."

Hubbard expresses the idea that progress and innovation often happen quickly. This quote encourages a mindset of possibility and action in the face of challenges.

Elbert Hubbard was the founder of the Roycroft artisan community and a proponent of the Arts and Crafts Movement. His writings often focused on topics such as productivity, individualism, and the pursuit of personal excellence.

William James

William James

William James, a pioneer in the realm of self-help and personal development, emerges as an author of profound significance. His body of work stands as a testament to both remarkable accomplishments and a dedicated pursuit of fostering substantial growth in readers. Through his writings, James skillfully navigates the intricacies of the human experience, offering a wealth of insights and principles that serve as a compass for personal transformation and development.

What distinguishes James as an author is not only the brilliance of his ideas but also his keen understanding of the human psyche. His work goes beyond the confines of traditional literature, becoming a transformative force that empowers readers to embark on journeys of self-discovery and improvement. James's achievements extend beyond the written word, reflecting a commitment to providing readers with the tools they need to cultivate lives of enduring value.

In exploring the depths of James's work, one encounters a reservoir of wisdom that resonates with individuals seeking to navigate the complexities of self-help and personal growth. His writings become not just sources of information but trusted companions on the path to self-improvement, offering invaluable guidance and actionable insights to those striving to enhance the quality of their lives.

The legacy of William James transcends temporal boundaries, making his work a timeless source of inspiration for successive generations. His exceptional contributions as an author continue to be a wellspring of empowerment, equipping readers with the means to navigate the intricate journey of self-help and personal development.

William James's impact endures, and his work remains a beacon guiding individuals toward a life of greater purpose and value.

Mastering Success through William James's "The Energies of Men"

In his groundbreaking work, "The Energies of Men," William James extends a compelling invitation to explore the intricate dimensions of the human spirit and the latent reservoirs of energy within. While the book doesn't explicitly delve into the realms of positive thinking and goal setting, it subtly intertwines principles that later became foundational in the field of self-help literature.

The narrative unfolds as a guide to understanding and harnessing the untapped energies residing within individuals. James encourages readers to discern the latent potential within themselves, fostering a narrative that speaks to the resilience and vitality lying dormant in the human psyche.

Woven into this exploration is the notion of positive energy, subtly emphasizing the transformative impact of maintaining a positive mindset on overall energy and mental fortitude. Though not explicitly labeled as such, the book serves as a precursor to the principles of positive thinking, highlighting the profound benefits of cultivating a positive outlook.

While not overtly focused on goal setting, the narrative lays the groundwork for a profound understanding of personal growth. James prompts readers to contemplate the direction of their energies and the pursuit of endeavors aligned with their deepest aspirations. He encourages individuals to harness their inner potential and channel their energies towards meaningful goals, setting the stage for a life of purpose and fulfillment.

"The Energies of Men" emerges as a foundational text for later self-help literature, indirectly guiding readers toward recognizing inner potential, fostering positive thinking, and setting the stage for goal-oriented living. James's insights stand as a timeless source of inspiration for those seeking to unlock their inner reservoirs of energy and embark on a journey of personal transformation.

beyond its psychological exploration, "The Energies of Men" becomes a roadmap for readers to tap into latent energies, embrace positive thinking, and lay the foundation for goal-oriented living. William James's work continues to echo as a timeless guide for infusing life with renewed vitality and purpose, empowering individuals to unleash their inner strength and achieve their full potential.

William James's Principles of Success

William James, a renowned figure in the fields of philosophy and psychology, imparts a profound and enduring success principle—the Principle of Habit. At the heart of James's philosophy lies the idea that our habits, the actions we engage in regularly, shape the course of our lives, and, consequently, our success. He contends that genuine success is not merely a result of extraordinary achievements but rather the cumulative effect of daily habits and choices.

James encourages individuals to recognize the profound impact of habits on their thought patterns, actions, and ultimately, the trajectory of their lives. He argues that cultivating positive habits, small yet consistent, contributes significantly to personal development and success. This principle underscores the transformative power of habitual behaviors on the overall quality of life.

The Principle of Habit emerges as a cornerstone for those seeking success, prompting individuals to assess and refine their daily routines. By instilling positive habits, James asserts that individuals can navigate challenges more effectively, foster a growth mindset, and lay the foundation for enduring success. This principle, timeless in its applicability, extends beyond mere achievement and resonates with the broader pursuit of a fulfilling and purposeful life.

William James's Principle of Habit remains a guiding beacon for individuals aspiring to achieve lasting success. It serves as a profound reminder that the seemingly mundane choices we make daily wield tremendous influence, shaping the contours of our lives and propelling us toward a future defined by accomplishment and personal fulfillment.

Quote

"The greatest use of life is to spend it for something that will outlast it."

James emphasizes the idea of a meaningful and enduring impact. This quote suggests that dedicating one's life to something larger than oneself is a valuable and fulfilling pursuit.

"Act as if what you do makes a difference. It does."

This quote encourages individuals to recognize the significance of their actions, no matter how small. James emphasizes the power of personal agency and the ripple effect of individual contributions.

"Believe that life is worth living and your belief will help create the fact."

James underscores the role of belief and attitude in shaping one's experiences. This quote suggests that a positive outlook can contribute to a fulfilling and worthwhile life.

William James made significant contributions to psychology, philosophy, and the study of human consciousness. His pragmatic approach emphasized the practical consequences of beliefs and ideas, and he had a profound impact on the development of American thought in the late 19th and early 20th centuries.

Booker T. Washington

Booker T. Washington

Booker T. Washington stands as an exceptional author, celebrated for his remarkable work and profound contributions to the realm of self-help and personal development. His literary legacy is not merely a collection of words but a transformative force that seeks to cultivate significant growth in readers, providing valuable insights and principles to navigate the journey of self-improvement.

Washington's authorship transcends the confines of conventional literature, evolving into a guiding light for individuals navigating the intricate landscapes of self-help and personal development. His achievements extend beyond accolades, resonating in a visionary dedication to empowering readers, fostering a narrative that encourages enduring growth and personal enrichment.

What distinguishes Washington as an exceptional author is not only the brilliance of his ideas but also his unique ability to forge a profound connection with readers. His works become more than mere texts; they evolve into companions on the journey of self-improvement, offering wisdom, encouragement, and actionable guidance to those striving to enhance the quality of their lives.

Washington's legacy is not bound to a specific era; it resonates through time, inspiring generations with a timeless message of perseverance, self-reliance, and the pursuit of personal excellence. His work remains a source of guidance for those striving to unlock their true potential and lead lives of purpose, enriched by the valuable principles embedded in Washington's writings.

Booker T. Washington's contributions as an exceptional author represent a legacy of empowerment and enlightenment. His remarkable work continues to be a wellspring of inspiration, providing readers with the tools they need to navigate the journey of self-help and personal development, fostering a legacy of growth that extends far beyond the pages of his writings.

Mastering Success through Booker T. Washington's "Up from Slavery"

In his inspirational autobiography "Up from Slavery," Booker T. Washington paints a compelling narrative of triumph over adversity, revealing the transformative power of positive thinking and goal setting. Beyond a mere account of his personal life, the book becomes a testament to resilience, with Washington's early life in slavery serving as a backdrop for a story that underscores the strength derived from maintaining a positive mindset in the face of formidable challenges.

Woven throughout the narrative is the theme of positive thinking as a catalyst for change. Washington's unwavering optimism and belief in progress become foundational principles that echo through the corridors of self-help wisdom. His remarkable journey from enslavement to education stands as a testament to the transformative potential of maintaining a positive outlook on life, demonstrating that even in the face of immense obstacles, a positive mindset can be a powerful force for personal growth and achievement.

The autobiography unfolds as a roadmap for goal setting, particularly in the realm of education. Washington's unwavering commitment to acquiring knowledge becomes a pivotal element in his narrative, emphasizing the importance of setting clear goals as a means of transcending limitations and shaping a brighter future. He eloquently demonstrates that education serves as a powerful tool for empowerment, enabling individuals to break free from the shackles of adversity and pursue a path of personal fulfillment.

"Up from Slavery" emerges as a precursor to later self-help literature by exemplifying the transformative power of positive thinking and goal setting. Washington's insights extend beyond his personal story, becoming universal principles that resonate with individuals seeking to navigate their paths of self-improvement. the book serves as an enduring testament to the power of the human spirit, offering timeless guidance for those on the journey of self-help and personal development. It remains a beacon of hope, inspiring generations to embrace the transformative power of optimism, perseverance, and a steadfast commitment to personal growth.

Booker T. Washington's Principles of Success

Booker T. Washington, a beacon of wisdom and resilience, imparts a timeless success principle encapsulated in the concept of self-help through education. His indomitable spirit and life's work advocate for the transformative power of learning and self-improvement as the keys to individual success.

Washington's principle revolves around the empowering idea that education is the cornerstone of personal and collective progress. He encourages individuals to empower themselves through the acquisition of knowledge and skills, transcending societal constraints and prejudice. His unwavering belief in the power of education as a tool for self-elevation resonates through generations, marking it as a fundamental success principle that has stood the test of time.

In the face of adversity, Washington championed the philosophy of self-help, promoting the notion that individuals could uplift themselves through education and industriousness. This principle echoes not only as a strategy for personal advancement but also as a means to contribute positively to society, fostering a legacy of resilience and self-determination. It serves as a reminder that even in the face of challenges, individuals have the power to shape their own destinies.

Furthermore, Washington's success principle underscores the importance of practical education, aligning skills and knowledge with real-world applications. By advocating for a balance between academic pursuits and hands-on experience, he positions education as a dynamic force capable of unlocking doors to prosperity and self-sufficiency. This practical approach to education ensures that individuals acquire the skills and knowledge necessary to not only succeed in their chosen fields but also contribute meaningfully to society.

Booker T. Washington's invaluable success principle centers on self-help through education—an enduring philosophy that encourages individuals to seize control of their destinies, overcome obstacles, and contribute meaningfully to the betterment of themselves and society as a whole. His unwavering belief in the power of education continues to inspire generations, empowering individuals to break free from the shackles of adversity and pursue their dreams.

Quote

"Success is to be measured not so much by the position that one has reached in life as by the obstacles which he has overcome."

Washington emphasizes the idea that true success is determined by the challenges one has overcome rather than just the outward achievements or social status.

"I have learned that success is to be measured not so much by the position that one has reached in life as by the obstacles which he has had to overcome while trying to succeed."

This quote reiterates Washington's belief in the importance of overcoming obstacles and challenges on the path to success.

"You measure the size of the accomplishment by the obstacles you had to overcome to reach your goals."

Washington's perspective on success is once again highlighted in this quote, emphasizing that the significance of an accomplishment is measured by the difficulties and obstacles one has faced and conquered.

Booker T. Washington was a prominent advocate for vocational and industrial education for African Americans and played a key role in the early development of historically black colleges and universities. His philosophy and leadership had a lasting impact on the African American community in the late 19th and early 20th centuries.

P.T. Barnum

P.T. Barnum

P.T. Barnum, an engaging author and innovator, leaves a lasting impact with his remarkable work that goes beyond entertainment into self-help and personal growth. Renowned for his mastery in showmanship and engaging audiences, Barnum's writings as an author delve deeper, providing readers insights beyond the spectacle.

Barnum's noteworthy achievements are not limited to entertainment; they serve as a foundation for meaningful development in readers. His work becomes a source of valuable lessons, guiding people on a transformative self-help journey.

Core to Barnum's philosophy is nurturing one's distinctive talents and skills. Drawing from his entertainment experiences, he encourages readers to recognize and develop their unique strengths, enabling self-discovery and growth.

Additionally, Barnum's work stresses adaptability and resilience. Despite difficulties, he advocates turning adversity into opportunity - showcasing a mindset critical for personal advancement. His writing motivates by inspiring optimism and determination when navigating life's twists and turns.

Barnum's legacy reaches past the big top tent - it becomes a reservoir of wisdom for those pursuing life proficiencies. His work reminds that personal progress is not a fixed target but an evolving expedition, where embracing uniqueness and resilience are vital components.

P.T. Barnum's literary contributions resonate as a source of motivation and guidance for meaningful self-help and development. His exceptional work affirms the enduring worth of nurturing talent, persevering with resilience, and relishing the extraordinary adventure of transformation.

Mastering Success through P.T. Barnum's "The Art of Money Getting"

In "The Art of Money Getting," famed entrepreneur P.T. Barnum shares enduring wisdom that reaches beyond his era. This insightful text transcends financial success, becoming a guide to mastering life's art. Barnum's words resound with the might of positive thinking, urging readers to harness mental strength to shape their destiny. He fervently argues that a positive mindset is the bedrock of any triumph, a tenet resonating through time.

The pages reveal the secrets of goal-setting, unveiling them as the compass to navigate life's uncertain journey. Barnum imparts practical advice on crafting achievable goals, underscoring their import in the quest for success. His teachings chart the course, steering individuals away from indecision's pitfalls toward purposeful living.

As we delve deeper, Barnum's profundity becomes clear - seeds of insight that blossomed into self-help's vast forest. The positive thinking and goal-setting fundamentals underpinning "The Art of Money Getting" laid the groundwork for countless principles that followed. Still today, these learnings continue empowering people worldwide.

In this summary, we distill Barnum's resonant teachings, inviting readers to imbibe the transformative might of positivity and intentional goal-setting. "The Art of Money Getting" endures not as a relic but a timeless guide, unlocking a mindset beyond wealth toward fulfillment and lasting achievement.

Through P.T. Barnum's Principles of Success

Embedded within P.T. Barnum's teachings gleams success tenets illuminating the path for aspiring individuals.

Core to his wisdom is a steadfast belief in optimism's power. Barnum asserts that maintaining a positive mindset is not just preferable but a strategic choice that can remake one's reality. The principle is straightforward yet profound: thoughts architect our destiny. By cultivating an upbeat outlook, one navigates life's hurdles with poise while attracting successes like a magnet.

Barnum's precept extends beyond mere positivity; it takes root in intentional goal-setting. He recognizes dreams sans plans as fleeting fantasies. Thus, he urges meticulously crafting clear, viable goals - lighthouses amid storms, providing direction and purpose. The principle calls people to define aspirations clearly then work tirelessly towards actualization.

Adaptability is another pillar of Barnum's philosophy. He accepts change's inevitability and holds that success belongs to those pivot gracefully when met with adversity. In Barnum's view, flexibility is not compromise but a strategic maneuver to stay ahead amid life's dynamic dance.

P.T. Barnum's most valuable success tenet is a holistic fusion of positive thinking, deliberate goal-setting, and resilient adaptability. It is a timeless recipe for achievement, echoing beyond "The Art of Money Getting" as a guiding mantra for those daring to dream and striving toward greatness.

Quote

"The noblest art is that of making others happy."

Barnum expressed his belief in the value of bringing joy and happiness to others. This quote reflects his perspective on the positive impact of entertainment and the arts.

"Every crowd has a silver lining."

This quote plays on the familiar phrase "every cloud has a silver lining," suggesting that in the context of entertainment and showmanship, every gathering or audience presents an opportunity for success and positivity.

"The foundation of success in life is good health: that is the substratum fortune; it is also the basis of happiness. A person cannot accumulate a fortune very well when he is sick."

Barnum recognized the importance of good health as a foundational element for success and happiness. This quote underscores the connection between well-being and the ability to pursue one's goals.

P.T. Barnum is best known for founding the Barnum & Bailey Circus and for his skill in promoting and marketing various forms of entertainment. His contributions to the world of entertainment and showmanship have left a lasting legacy.

William Walker Atkinson

William Walker Atkinson

William Walker Atkinson, a luminary in self-help and personal growth, left an indelible impact on human potential's landscape. His exceptional work, spanning the late 19th and early 20th centuries, remains a wellspring of wisdom for those pursuing personal empowerment.

One of Atkinson's significant contributions was distilling esoteric knowledge into accessible, practical principles. Writing often under pseudonyms like Yogi Ramacharaka, he illuminated the path to self-discovery and actualization. Atkinson's teachings bridged the mystical and pragmatic, offering readers profound insights paired with actionable steps toward transformation.

One notable achievement was emphasizing the mind's power in shaping one's reality. Atkinson recognized thoughts' influence on individual circumstances, presaging a cornerstone of positive psychology. His work urged readers to harness mental faculties constructively, unlocking latent potential within.

Moreover, Atkinson's writings laid the groundwork for understanding the law of attraction – the notion that our thoughts and emotions shape the universe's response, underscoring positivity's import in manifesting outcomes.

In self-help literature's vast tapestry, Atkinson's legacy endures as a catalyst for reader transformation. Synthesizing ancient wisdom with contemporary resonance created a roadmap for those navigating personal growth's intricate journey.

The ripple effect of his work is evident in countless individuals experiencing significant mindset and tangible growth by applying his principles.

William Walker Atkinson stands as a pioneer whose contributions transcend time. His remarkable work not only enriched self-help and personal development but remains a source of inspiration for those embarking on self-discovery and empowerment.

Mastering Success through William Walker Atkinson's "Thought Vibration or the Law of Attraction in the Thought World"

Within the literary halls of "Thought Vibration or the Law of Attraction in the Thought World," William Walker Atkinson unfurls a captivating exploration into the mind's realm and its influence on reality. Published at the turn of the 20th century, this timeless work serves as a compass for understanding and harnessing thoughts' power.

In this insightful volume, Atkinson delves into the intricate interplay between thoughts and the universe, laying the bedrock for the later "law of attraction" concept. The book is a masterclass in deliberately directing thought vibrations to shape one's reality. While rooted in period language, Atkinson's prose resonates with a universal truth transcending eras – the profound impact of thoughts on life's unfolding tapestry.

Central to Atkinson's teachings is positive thinking, a notion that would become foundational in subsequent self-help literature. He conveys that cultivating an upbeat mental attitude is not just desirable but a dynamic force drawing in positive circumstances while repelling negativity. "Thought Vibration" becomes a manual for intentional living, guiding readers to navigate the thought-world purposefully.

Atkinson's exploration extends to goal-setting – a theme intertwining seamlessly with positivity's power. He elucidates transforming mental desires into tangible realities, underscoring focused thought and unwavering belief's role in achieving aspirations. The book charts the course for those seeking not just success but deeper comprehension of thought and manifestation's intricate interplay.

In this summary, we distill Atkinson's resonant teachings, inviting readers on a journey of self-discovery and empowerment. "Thought Vibration" shines as a beacon, illuminating the path to a life shaped by deliberate thoughts, positive vibrations, and transformative principles that continue reverberating through self-help literature.

William Walker Atkinson's Principles of Success

At the crux of William Walker Atkinson's profound teachings lies a timeless success tenet—one crossing eras' boundaries and resonating with individuals' universal quest for fulfillment. A self-help and metaphysics pioneer, Atkinson ardently promoted constructive thinking's transformative power.

His most valuable principle distills into consciously creating through thought. Atkinson's ideas posit the mind as not merely passive but an active force shaping one's reality contours. He stresses cultivating a positive mental attitude, arguing thoughts send ripples into the vast universal ocean, influencing manifesting circumstances.

Atkinson's precept underscores that success is not solely external but reflects internal thought and belief landscapes. He encourages individuals to become destiny architects by intentionally directing thoughts toward positive, constructive ends. This tenet becomes a guiding light for navigating complexities, urging people to harness inherent mental power for sculpting aspiration-aligned realities.

Moreover, Atkinson's principle extends beyond positivity to encompass deliberate, focused goal-setting. He articulates clearly defining objectives and maintaining staunch belief in their realization. This duo of optimism and purposeful goals creates synergy that propels actualization.

William Walker Atkinson's most valuable success motto encapsulates the notion that achievement results from thoughtful intent and deliberate action. It invites recognizing the transformative potential within our minds, wielding thoughts as tools for molding purposeful, abundant, and fulfilling lives. This principle, embedded in his teachings, remains a timeless beacon for those on personal and professional success journeys.

Quote

"The law of attraction is the law of love, and it is the law by which improvement is accomplished through natural agencies. [...] As a man thinketh in his heart, so is he."

Atkinson's quote reflects the New Thought philosophy, emphasizing the power of positive thinking and the idea that thoughts shape one's reality.

"Remember, no more effort is required to aim high in life, to demand abundance and prosperity, than is required to accept misery and poverty."

This quote encourages individuals to set high aspirations for themselves, suggesting that it takes no more effort to strive for success than it does to accept a less desirable situation.

"The mind, ever the willing servant, will respond to boldness, for boldness, in effect, is a command to deliver mental resources."

Atkinson highlights the role of confidence and assertiveness in harnessing the power of the mind. This quote suggests that a bold and assertive mindset can lead to the mobilization of mental resources.

William Walker Atkinson's writings often focused on the principles of mentalism, the power of thought, and the idea that individuals can shape their destinies through their mental attitudes and beliefs.

❁❁❁

Andrew Carnegie

Andrew Carnegie

Andrew Carnegie, an industrial titan during the Gilded Age, left an indelible impact not just on steel but on self-help and personal growth. His remarkable work reaches beyond machinery and furnaces into the human psyche – where Carnegie's insights continue to foster empowerment.

Carnegie's most renowned self-help contribution is perhaps "The Gospel of Wealth," encapsulating his philosophy on fortunes and moral obligation. In this seminal essay, he challenges conventions by proposing the wealthy should utilize assets to benefit society. This principle, rooted in philanthropy and responsibility, laid the groundwork for a broader success concept – one transcending personal wealth to encompass improving others' wellbeing.

Furthermore, Carnegie's self-help legacy intricately weaves with his success tenets. He believed in continuous self-improvement and skill building. His famous phrase "The man who dies rich dies disgraced" reflects not just disdain for idle affluence but endorsement of personal development and societal betterment.

Carnegie's journey from penniless immigrant to wealth exemplifies his principles. His compelling narrative illustrates self-help and growth potential within individuals.

Andrew Carnegie's remarkable achievements reach beyond industry. His self-help legacy serves as a beacon for accumulating wealth ethically and channeling it to advance humanity. Carnegie's philosophy underscores that true success measures positive societal impact – a valuable lesson continuing to inspire personal and collective growth.

Mastering Success through Andrew Carnegie's "The Gospel of Wealth"

Within "The Gospel of Wealth's" enduring pages, Andrew Carnegie pens a manifesto transcending wealth accumulation to offer profound guidance toward purposeful, responsible living. Published in 1889, this seminal work is not merely a treatise on amassing fortunes; it is a philosophical cornerstone echoing through self-help literature corridors.

In this illuminating volume, Carnegie challenges prevailing wealth notions by introducing responsible capitalism. He argues the affluent have a moral obligation to utilize riches for society's greater welfare. This foundational philanthropic ethos becomes a precursor to modern success conceptualization – an evolving narrative reaching beyond personal gain toward one's broader world impact.

At Carnegie's principles' heart lies a belief in positive thinking's transformative power. While the term may not be explicit, the underlying philosophy advocates cultivating a mindset seeing wealth not as an end but as means to contribute to others' wellbeing. Carnegie's gospel becomes a call to adopt a constructive perspective – where prosperity measures not solely by financial metrics but by the positive influence on people's lives.

Furthermore, the book subtly weaves the import of intentional goal-setting as Carnegie charts the course for aligning assets with purpose. He endorses continuous self-improvement and knowledge pursuit, emphasizing that success is not static but a dynamic growth and contribution journey.

In this summary, we distill "The Gospel of Wealth's" essence, inviting readers to explore positive thinking and purpose-driven goals' transformative might. Though rooted in the late 1800s, Carnegie's principles resonate timelessly to guide personal development's intricate terrain. The gospel echoes, urging individuals to harness their wealth, be it material or intellectual, as a force bettering humanity.

Andrew Carnegie's Principles of Success

At Andrew Carnegie's philosophy's nucleus lies a principle transcending mere wealth accumulation - the profound concept of responsible stewardship. Carnegie's most valuable success tenet, articulated in "The Gospel of Wealth," is that great affluence bears even greater responsibility to contribute positively.

Carnegie challenges the notion of amassing fortune as an end, proposing instead that the prosperous are trustees obligated to employ assets for the greater good. This responsible capitalism principle underscores one's transformative capacity to leverage wealth not as personal possession but a societal betterment tool. Carnegie's vision invites viewing success holistically, where financial prosperity becomes means to a noble end.

Moreover, Carnegie's principle advocates aligning personal accomplishments with broader purpose. He encourages adopting a positive mindset, recognizing that wealth and success allow non-zero-sum gains - positive thinking propels achievements benefiting both self and collective wellbeing.

The essence of Carnegie's motto extends beyond philanthropy - it becomes a call to intentional living and continuous self-improvement. The pursuit of knowledge and personal growth serves as a compass guiding the success journey. Carnegie's own ascent from humble immigrant to titan exemplifies this principle - his commitment to learning and development marking the path.

Carnegie's most valuable success principle invites seeing triumph not as isolated but profoundly impactful. By embracing responsible stewardship, cultivating positivity, and aligning with higher purpose, individuals can forge legacies of positive world influence beyond personal prosperity. Carnegie's motto remains a timeless beacon, inspiring striving that extends beyond self to leave an enduring human tapestry mark.

Quote

"The man who dies rich, dies disgraced."

Carnegie believed in the importance of philanthropy and giving back to society. This quote suggests that accumulating wealth without using it for the betterment of others is a dishonorable outcome.

"People who are unable to motivate themselves must be content with mediocrity, no matter how impressive their other talents."

Carnegie emphasizes the significance of self-motivation in achieving success. This quote suggests that without the drive to propel oneself forward, even exceptional talents may lead to mediocre outcomes.

"Do your duty and a little more, and the future will take care of itself."

Carnegie advocated for a strong sense of duty and responsibility. This quote suggests that by fulfilling one's obligations and going above and beyond, individuals can contribute to a positive and successful future.

Andrew Carnegie's legacy extends beyond his business success; he is perhaps equally well-known for his philanthropic endeavors, including the funding of libraries, education, and various cultural institutions. His commitment to giving back has had a lasting impact on society.

Charles F. Haanel

Charles F. Haanel

Charles F. Haanel, a self-help and personal development pioneer, etched his name into transformative literature's annals with his seminal work "The Master Key System." Published in the early 20th century, Haanel's enduring and profound contribution to personal growth remains indelible.

At Haanel's philosophy's crux lies a belief in the mind's power to shape one's destiny. "The Master Key System" serves as a guide to unlock individuals' latent potential and illuminate the path to self-discovery. Haanel's work is not merely motivational anecdotes; it is a systematic approach to comprehending the intricate connection between thought, consciousness, and manifesting desired outcomes.

One notable Haanel achievement is emphasizing the law of attraction - a concept gaining widespread recognition in later decades. He explores the idea of thoughts as vibrational frequencies resonating with the universe's energy to influence life's unfolding circumstances. Haanel's teachings became fundamental for harnessing this law toward personal and professional success.

Furthermore, Haanel's work extends into practical goal setting and achievement. He provides readers a systematic methodology for defining and realizing objectives, underscoring clarity, focus, and persistent effort's import. Although rooted in the early 1900s, his principles laid the groundwork for contemporary goal-setting approaches within self-help.

Charles F. Haanel's remarkable work demonstrates the mind's transformative might. His systematic framework, encompassing attraction laws and goal-setting, has provided a valuable self-discovery roadmap. Haanel's enduring legacy remains a source of inspiration, offering timeless wisdom to those seeking significant growth and fulfillment.

Mastering Success through Charles F. Haanel's "The Master Key System"

Within "The Master Key System," Charles F. Haanel unveils a transformative personal development blueprint echoing through self-help literature since its early 20th century publication. This groundbreaking work not only delves into the mind's intricacies but serves as a foundational text for positive thinking and goal-setting principles shaping the self-help landscape for generations.

Haanel's masterstroke is exploring positive thinking's power - an idea going beyond mere optimism into conscious creation's realm. He contends thoughts possess vibrational frequencies resonating with the universe's energy to influence life circumstances. "The Master Key System" becomes a manual for harnessing thoughts' creative power, emphasizing maintaining a positive mental attitude's profound impact.

Embedded is the law of attraction principle - a concept gaining mainstream recognition in later self-help works. Haanel introduces the notion of like attracting like, urging readers to align thoughts with desires for attracting positive outcomes. Articulated precisely in Haanel's book, this became a cornerstone for exploring dynamics between consciousness and manifestation.

Furthermore, Haanel provides a systematic goal-setting and achievement approach, emphasizing clearly defining objectives coupled with unwavering focus and persistent effort. These principles, though articulated in the early 1900s, laid the groundwork for contemporary goal-setting methodologies and time management techniques.

In this summary, we distill Haanel's resonant teachings inviting readers to explore the profound principles of positive thinking and goal-setting embedded in "The Master Key System." With timeless wisdom, the book serves as a guiding light for those on self-discovery journeys, offering transformative insights continually shaping the self-help genre.

Charles F. Haanel's Principles of Success

At "The Master Key System's" transformative teachings' crux lies Charles F. Haanel's resonant success principle—one transcending time's confines to guide those seeking fulfillment. Haanel's most profound insight recognizes thought's creative power.

Haanel contends thoughts are not fleeting but dynamic forces shaping reality's fabric. This principle underscores the transformative potential within each mind - the ability to consciously direct thoughts toward desired outcomes. The tenet's core understands the mind as a powerful tool; by mastering positive thinking, individuals can unlock success's doors.

The principle delves deeper than positivity affirmation into deliberate reality creation. Haanel invites readers to recognize the causal thoughts-to-circumstances relationship and become destiny's architects by cultivating positivity and aligning with desired outcomes.

Moreover, Haanel's motto resonates with the law of attraction - gaining later self-help prominence. He encourages understanding that thought energy attracts similar universal energies to manifest aspirations. By embracing this, one can harness forces to achieve aims.

Charles F. Haanel's most valuable success principle recognizes the mind's powerful creative capacity. By embracing positive thinking's might and the dynamics between thoughts and reality, individuals can embark on intentional, purposeful journeys. Haanel's enduring legacy remains a timeless reminder that success stems not just from external actions but from deliberately nurtured mental patterns.

Quote

"The world without is a reflection of the world within. What appears without is what has been found within."

Haanel's quote emphasizes the idea that external circumstances are a reflection of one's internal thoughts and beliefs. It aligns with the concept that our mindset and consciousness shape our experiences.

"The only thing which can bind us is the law of belief."

Haanel highlights the power of belief in shaping our reality. According to this quote, our beliefs have the potential to either limit or empower us, influencing the outcomes we experience.

"All possession is the result of the accumulative attitude of mind, or the money consciousness; this is the magic wand which will enable you to receive the idea, and it will formulate plans for you to execute."

This quote underscores the importance of a positive and abundance-focused mindset in achieving success and acquiring possessions. Haanel suggests that a wealth-conscious mentality is a key factor in attracting prosperity.

Charles F. Haanel's best-known work is "The Master Key System," a personal development book that has influenced many in the self-help and New Thought movements. His teachings often revolve around the power of the mind, visualization, and the law of attraction.

❁❁❁

George S. Clason

George S. Clason

George S. Clason, a personal finance and self-help pioneer, carved an enduring legacy with his seminal work "The Richest Man in Babylon." Published in 1926, Clason's insightful parables have become a timeless guide for financial wisdom and profound self-development insights.

Clason's achievement lies in distilling ancient wealth principles into engaging ancient Babylon stories. Through tales of the wise and prosperous, he imparts enduring financial success fundamentals. Each narrative serves as a conduit to explore not just wealth-building mechanics but also deeper self-discipline, integrity, and conscious decision-making.

"The Richest Man in Babylon" stands out for its simplicity and applicability. Clason transcends financial complexity by offering straightforward, cross-generational advice. His accomplishment is crafting a literary masterpiece seamlessly integrating finance with personal growth.

At its essence, Clason's work emphasizes personal responsibility and disciplined financial habits' transformative potential. The principles outlined extend beyond money management as foundational self-improvement pillars. The path to prosperity, as charted by Clason, intertwines with the journey toward mindful self-discovery.

George S. Clason's remarkable work reaches beyond conventional finance literature. "The Richest Man in Babylon" illuminates not just financial success but personal development and self-help avenues. Clason's timeless wisdom continues guiding and inspiring enriched, fulfilling growth.

Mastering Success through George S. Clason's "The Richest Man in Babylon"

In ancient Babylon, George S. Clason weaves enduring financial wisdom into "The Richest Man in Babylon." Published in 1926, this literary masterpiece transcends its era to offer not just financial success but a personal growth and self-help roadmap.

Through captivating ancient Babylonian parables, Clason imparts age-old principles laying modern self-help literature's foundation. At these tales' crux lies positive thinking – propelling characters from financial ignorance to prosperity's pinnacle. The notion of thoughts shaping one's destiny becomes a foundational theme, resonating as characters transform circumstances by shifting mindset.

Furthermore, Clason seamlessly integrates goal-setting's power, as characters embark on intentional wealth-building quests by setting clear objectives and working with determination. Principles become not just financial vehicles but personal growth catalysts.

As readers traverse Babylon's ancient streets through Clason's narratives, they encounter self-help fundamentals embedded in each tale. Characters grapple with discipline, integrity and conscious decision-making's potential. The book becomes a wisdom reservoir where pursuing fortunes intertwines with enriching, purposeful life journeys.

In this summary, we distill "Richest Man" essence, inviting readers to explore positive thinking and goal-setting's power as cornerstones for financial and personal success. Clason's work bridges the ages, offering timeless insights continuing to guide and inspire significant life growth.

George S. Clason's Principles of Success

At the crux of George S. Clason's enduring wisdom in "The Richest Man in Babylon" lies a timeless success principle transcending financial prosperity – the art of disciplined wealth-building. Clason's masterpiece guides readers not just toward financial triumphs but imparts principles crucial for personal growth.

The most valuable principle woven into Clason's narratives is steadfast commitment to saving and investing. Through Babylon's characters, he underscores disciplined money management's mighty potential, via a simple yet profound motto – systematically set aside earnings portions for future-building, regardless of modesty. This cornerstone tenet propels journeys from struggle to affluence.

Clason's emphasis on disciplined wealth-building extends beyond practical finances into a metaphor for goal setting and intentional living. The characters embody the principle that success emerges not overnight but through consistent, purposeful actions. The path to prosperity, as Clason outlines, mirrors the broader personal growth trek.

Moreover, Clason's motto grounds in leveraging one's expertise for financial gains. Babylonians continuously improve through education, recognizing knowledge acquisition's instrumental role in wealth-creation, making this a clarion call for lifelong learning and skill building enabling professional and personal success.

George S. Clason's most valuable success principle transcends finance to encapsulate disciplined wealth-building, continuous self-improvement, and intentional knowledge pursuit's transformative power. As readers journey through ancient Babylon, they discover guiding philosophy that shapes not just financial destinies but significant growth in life's facets.

Clason's wisdom endures a beacon, inspiring purposeful navigation toward prosperity.

Quote

"Start thy purse to fattening."

This quote emphasizes the importance of saving and accumulating wealth gradually. Clason's teachings often revolve around the principles of sound financial management.

"Our acts can be no wiser than our thoughts."

Clason underscores the connection between thoughts and actions. This quote suggests that wise thinking is the foundation for wise decision-making and behavior.

"Make thy gold multiply."

This quote encourages the idea of investing and growing one's wealth. Clason advocates for making strategic financial decisions that lead to the multiplication of resources.

George S. Clason's "The Richest Man in Babylon" uses timeless financial principles presented in the form of parables to convey lessons on wealth-building and financial success. The book has been widely read and praised for its accessible and practical advice.

~The End~